VERY SIMPLE
ITALIAN

ILLUSTRATED BY
IRENE SANDERSON

VERY SIMPLE
ITALIAN

By
Hugh Shankland

Simple Books Ltd
Sandgate, Folkestone, Kent, England

VERY SIMPLE ITALIAN
Simple Books Ltd
Knoll House, 35 The Crescent, Sandgate, Folkestone,
Kent, England CT20 3EE

First published 1992
© Simple Books Ltd

ISBN 1-873411-25-1

British Library Cataloguing in Publication Data

**A CIP catalogue record for this book
is available from the British Library**

Distributed in the USA & Canada by:
The Talman Co. Inc.
131 Spring Street
New York, NY 10012
USA

Photoset in Souvenir Light 11 on 12pt
by Ashford Composition Ltd, Ashford, Kent
Printed in England by Hollen Street Press Ltd, Slough, Berks

Contents

Fontana del Nettuno

Foreword

One result of the extraordinary social and economic development of Italy since the end of World War II, along with the worldwide revolution in technology and communications, is that English is widely studied in Italian schools and English/American words are added almost daily to the Italian vocabulary. Even so, most Italians will tell you that they find English quite difficult to learn, and certainly it is very far from being universally spoken or understood in any depth at all.

Equally, most will be delighted to find you making a similar effort to use their language, and when you run out of inspiration you might well feel encouraged by their own inventiveness in dismissing the idea that linguistic limitations are an insurmountable barrier to communication!

Your difficulties will generally be greeted with patience and sympathy, not least because Italians have a considerable respect for the language, partly because so many have themselves also gone through the experience of acquiring 'good' Italian. It is not the first tongue of three-quarters of the population, who among their own kind speak a local dialect which in most cases is dramatically unlike the 'standard' Italian learned at school and used in the press and on television.

Here, of course, you are being introduced to the standard or national language of Italy which everyone now is able to converse in more or less comfortably, except for the elderly in the remotest areas and islands.

HUGH SHANKLAND

1

Introducing the Italian Language

..all things are either masculine or feminine

Italian has a very sophisticated grammar system, but simple points can be put across effectively without any profound knowledge of it. So do not feel intimidated. When embarking on a new language, the first need is to be bold, even experimental, and not to mind making a fool of yourself. How else would you learn?

There are a few points of grammar which I think are essential, and I will try to make them very simple to grasp. They all concern two basic principles of the Italian language. 1) all things are either masculine or feminine; 2) all verbs inflect; i.e. their final sounds vary according to the information which a verb has to convey.

This information principally concerns time (e.g. present time/past time), and 'persons'. Thus in 'I speak' the time is the present and the person is 'I'. A dictionary tells you 'speak' is *parlare*. You inflect *parlare* to make it mean 'I speak': *parlo*.

Take a pocket dictionary with you to Italy. There are plenty available at low cost. VERY SIMPLE ITALIAN teaches by giving helpful examples of the language in the kind of everyday situations which you are likely to face as soon as you are in Italy, or in Italian-speaking Switzerland.

Once you get the feel of these basic ways of saying, you can easily adapt them by substituting words found here with comparable new ones looked up in your dictionary. Fortunately for English speakers, innumerable Italian words are very easy to recognise and also memorise, because they have close equivalents in the English vocabulary. (See Chapter 7.)

MASCULINE AND FEMININE

Not only persons (*Anna, Giorgio*) but all other things (and all words referring to them) are either masculine or feminine. English does not make this distinction.

Masculine	**Feminine**
il giorno (the day)	*la sera* (the evening)
questo (this)	*questa* (this)
americano (American)	*americana* (American)
inglese (English)	*inglese* (English)
l'albergo (the hotel)	*l'Italia* (Italy)
il mio amico Giorgio	*la mia amica Anna*
(My friend George)	(My friend Ann)

Words (both nouns and adjectives) that end with 'o' are masculine. Words that end with 'a' are feminine. 'The' has masculine/feminine forms too: *il* (masculine), *la* (feminine), according to the gender of the word it accompanies: **il** *giorn***o**, **la** *ser***a**. But before a vowel 'the' is 'l' for either gender: **l'***albergo*, **l'***Italia*.

*Quest***o** *è* **il** *marito di Anna. È inglese.*
This is Anna's husband. He is English.
*Quest***a** *è* **la** *moglie di Giorgio. È americana.*
This is Giorgio's wife. She is American.

Moglie, like *inglese*, ends in 'e'. Some words ending in 'e' are masculine, some are feminine. *Inglese*, an adjective, can be both. Obviously 'wife' is feminine, but with a great many 'e'-ending words you will just have to guess (and learn!) whether '*il*' or '*la*' is correct. Examples:

il *mare* (the sea)
il *ristorante* (the restaurant)
la *notte* (the night)
la *televisione* (the television)

SINGULAR AND PLURAL

The general rule is that words ending in 'a' when singular change to 'e' when plural. Words ending in 'o' or 'e' change to 'i'. Note how *la* and *il* also have plural forms: *le* and *i*.

SINGULAR	PLURAL
*la past***a**	*le past***e**
*il cappuccin***o**	*i cappuccin***i**
*la decision***e**	*le decision***i**
*il limon***e**	*i limon***i**

SINGULAR	PLURAL
la *signor***a** *italian***a**	**le** *signor***e** *italian***e**
(the Italian lady)	(the Italian ladies)
la *signor***a** *ingle***se**	**le** *signor***e** *ingle***si**
(the English lady)	(the English ladies)
il *signor***e** *ingle***se**	**i** *signor***i** *ingle***si**
(the English man)	(the English men)
il *signor***e** *italian***o**	**i** *signor***i** *italian***i**
(the Italian man)	(the Italian men)

In front of a masculine word beginning with 's' before another consonant 'the' is *lo*. The plural is *gli*. The plural form of *l'* is also *gli*, if the word is masculine.

SINGULAR	PLURAL
lo straniero	*gli* stranieri
(the foreigner)	(the foreigners)
*l'*italiano	*gli* italiani
(the Italian)	(the Italians)

'A' or 'an' is *un* before a masculine word, but *uno* before a masculine word beginning with 's' before another consonant. It is *una* before a feminine word, shortened to *un'* if it begins with a vowel.

Examples:

un bicchiere	a glass
uno spuntino	a snack
una limonata	a lemonade
un' aranciata	an orangeade

VERBS (Present time)

I=**io** We=**noi** He=**lui** She=**lei** You=**lei**.
There is no word for 'it' in spoken Italian.

To say 'I …' the last sound is -**o**
To say 'We …' the last sound is -**iamo**
To say 'He …
'She …'
'You …'
'It …'
} the last sound of the verb is -**a** or -**e**

The dictionary only gives a verb in its simplest form — e.g. *arrivare*, to arrive; *prendere*, to take; *partire*, to leave. This is known as the 'infinitive' form of the verb. For other forms, the last part of the infinitive must be changed according to what you want the verb to say.

```
INFINITIVE
To …
1. arriv  ARE           arrive
2. prend  ERE           take
3. part   IRE           leave
PRESENT TIME
I …              We …            He/She/You/It …
1. arrivo          arriviAMO        arrivA
2. prendo          prendiAMO        prendE
3. parto           partiAMO         partE
```

Every Italian verb is placed in one of these three categories (conjugations) according to the way its infinitive form ends: -*are* -*ere* or -*ire*. For 'I …' and 'we …' all three verb types make identical changes. For 'he/she/you/it …' you have to learn to distinguish an -*are* verb from the other two types.

The 'persons'[†] are usually left out in Italian, since the change in the last part of the verb already carries sufficient information. Only use them for emphasis or clarification. Compare:

Partiamo.   We are leaving.

Noi partiamo, non lei.   We are leaving, not you.

Of course some confusion might arise in the case of 'he, she, you, it', since the ending of the verb is identical — and 'she' and 'you' are even the same word!

---

† The other persons are *loro* (they), and *tu* and *voi*, both of which translate 'you' in English. To address a person as *lei* rather than *tu* is the accepted norm in Italy among people who are not on intimate terms. *Tu* is becoming more acceptable, but is still largely felt to be very informal, commonly used among young people and closer acquaintances, people who would use *ciao* to each other as a greeting. *Voi* is used when you are addressing more than one person. These forms require different changes to the verb, and are not taught here.

(Lui) arriva	He arrives
(Lei) arriva	She arrives
(Lei) arriva	You arrive
arriva	It arrives

In practice, the context nearly always makes it perfectly clear who is the person implied:

Mia figlia è ancora in Inghilterra. Arriva domani.

My daughter is still in England. *She* arrives tomorrow.

Pronto, signor Pavarotti. Quando arriva a Roma?

Hello, Mr Pavarotti. When will *you* be arriving in Rome?

Notice how convenient it is that you can use the present of the verb to refer to something in the future.

VERBS (Past time)

a) with *AVERE*

Avere (to have): *io* **HO**=I have *noi* **ABBIAMO**=*we* have *lui, lei* **HA**=he, she, it has, you have

Examples:

1. *Ho **lavorato** molto.*	I (have) **worked** a lot.
2. *Abbiamo **avuto** una bella vacanza.*	We (have) **had** a lovely holiday.
3. *Ha **capito**.*	He (has) **understood**.

1. -ARE verbs change the ending to -ATO
(*lavorARE — lavorATO*)
2. -ERE verbs change the ending to -UTO
(*avERE — avUTO*)
3. -IRE verbs change the ending to -ITO
(*capIRE — capITO*)

Verb types 1 and 3 tend to be regular, but most type 2 verbs (in -ERE) are irregular, and so have to be learnt as they crop up. Here are two useful irregular pasts:

fare (to make) — **fatto** (made, done)
predere (to take) — **preso** (taken).

Ha **fatto** *buon viaggio?*	Did you have a good journey?
Sì, abbiamo **preso** *le cuccette.*	Yes, we took couchettes.

b) with *ESSERE*

Essere (to be): *io* **sono**=I am *noi* **siamo**=we are
lui, lei **è**=he, she, it is, you are

Examples:

Sono **stato/a** *in Italia.*	I have **been** to Italy.
Siamo **andati** *a Napoli.*	We **went** to Naples.
Mia figlia è **arrivata**	My daughter has **arrived**.

A few important verbs require *ESSERE* (instead of *avere*) when used in the past. Some of the most common include *essere* itself:

essere (to be) — **stato**
andare (to go) — **andato**
arrivare (to arrive) — **arrivato**
nascere (to be born) — **nato**
partire (to leave) — **partito**
venire (to come) — **venuto** (irregular).

Verbs used with *essere* agree with the person (the subject) i.e. are in feminine form if the person is feminine, plural if plural etc.

Mia sorella è arrivata ieri.
My sister arrived yesterday. (Feminine)
Il treno è arrivato a Roma due ore fa.
The train arrived at Rome two hours ago. (Masculine)

Siamo partiti da Milano a mezzanotte.
We left Milan at midnight. (Plural)
Le *ragazze sono state al mare.*
The girls have been at the seaside. (Feminine plural)

NEGATIVES

Not: *Non ...*
Nothing: *Non ... niente*
Never: *Non ... mai*
e.g. **Non** *bevo.*   I don't drink.
    Non *bevo* **niente.**   I drink nothing/don't drink anything.

    Non *bevo* **mai.**   I never drink.

2

Sounding Italian

A passable Italian accent is not hard to develop, if you concentrate on sounding every syllable clearly, and the five vowels correctly. Unlike in most forms of English, Italian vowels are not slurred but sounded roundly and clearly. Imitating native speakers is the best help you can get, but here are some indications.

a: 'ah' (very like English 'a' in 'path')
e: 'eh' (very like English 'e' in 'rent')
i: 'ee' (very like English 'i' in 'bikini')
o: 'oh' (very like English 'o' in 'order')
u: 'oo' (very like English 'u' in 'flute')

Examples: *italiano:* 'ee-tah-lee-AH-noh' (Italian)
Stati Uniti: 'STAH-tee OO-NEE-tee' (United States)

As you can see, written Italian very accurately records the way each syllable is spoken. But there are still a few conventions which you need to recognise in order to read Italian correctly. Nearly all concern the letters 'c', 'g' and 'h'. (Capitalised letters indicate where the stress falls).

'C' is a hard 'k' sound (like 'cat', 'cot', 'cut' in English), except before 'e' and 'i' when it is soft, i.e., sounded like 'ch' in English 'chest' and 'chin'. Examples: **Hard C:** *casa* (KAH-zah: house); *cosa* (KOH-zah: thing); *cubo* (KOO-boh: cube). **Soft C:** *cena* (CHEH-nah: supper); *concerto* (kon-CHEHR-toh: concert); *cibo* (CHEE-boh: food); *Francia* (FRAHN-chah: France); *bacio* (BAH-choh: kiss).

'G' is similarly pronounced hard before 'a' 'o' 'u' (like English 'gate', 'got', 'gut') and soft before 'e' and 'i' (as English 'gel' and 'gin'). Examples: **Hard G:** *gatto* (GAHT-toh: cat); *gusto* (GOO-stoh: taste); *pagare* (pah-GAH-ray). **Soft G:** *gelato* (jay-LAH-toh: ice cream); *gita* (JEE-tah: trip); *giovane* (JOH-vahn-neh: young).

'H' is never sounded in Italian ('Hotel' is pronounced 'Otell'). But **'h' combined with 'c' and 'g' has a special function.** It shows that a 'c' or 'g' must be sounded **hard not soft,** as you see in the cases of 'orchestra' and 'spaghetti'. Other examples: *chilo* (KEE-loh: kilo); *Michele* (Mee-KAY-lay: Michael); *chiesa* (kee-EH-zah: church); *laghi* (LAH-ghee: lakes).

Other letter combinations:
  'GN' is like the 'ny' in 'canyon': *bagno* (BAN-yoh: bath), *campagna* (kam-PAN-yah: countryside).
  'GL' is like the 'll' in 'million': *bottiglia* (bot-TEE-lyah: bottle), *bagaglio* (bah-GAH-lyoh: baggage).

'SCE' is like 'she' in 'shell': *scemo* (SHEH-moh: idiotic); *scena* (SHEH-nah: scene).

'SCI' is like 'shee' in 'sheep': *uscita* (oo-SHEE-tah: exit) *piscina* (pee-SHEE-nah: swimming pool).

A lso note:
'R' is lightly rolled when single (*Roma*), quite strongly trilled when double (*terra*). Don't worry too much if you can't do it, many North Italians can't or don't!

'S' in the middle of a word sounds like 'z': *rosa* (ROH-zah: rose), *sposo* (SPOH-zoh: spouse).

'U' before another vowel sounds like 'w': *Uomo* (WOH-moh: man); *buono* (BWOH-noh: good), *quando* (KWAHN-doh: when), *qui* (KWEE: here).

'ZZ' in the middle of a word sounds like 'ts': *Pazzo* (PAT-soh: crazy); *ragazza* (rah-GAT-sah: girl).

STRESS

W ords are usually stressed on the second-to last syllable (*italiano*). Quite often the stress falls earlier (*magnifico*: magnificent), and very occasionally on the last syllable (*città*: city). Only in the last case is an accent actually written.

T hroughout these pages, a letter underlined shows where an unusual stress falls in a word, i.e. when NOT the second-to-last syllable. Note that with words ending in -ia the stress normally falls on the next-to-last syllable, that is the 'i': *trattoria*, *farmacia*, *polizia*. But with words ending -io it normally falls earlier: *negozio*, *orario*, *bagaglio*. Also note that the words for the 'persons' are all stressed on the first vowel: *io*, *noi*, *lui*, *lei*.

3

Meeting Italians

Greetings

For 'hello' say *buon giorno* (good morning, good day). But from late afternoon onwards use *buona sera* (good afternoon, good evening). An all-purpose greeting is *salve!* (Hi there!).

Salve. Come sta?	Hello. How are you?
Bene, grazie.	Fine, thank you.
E lei?	And you?
Molto bene, grazie.	Very well, thank you.

When introducing someone, you say *Le presento ...* (May I introduce ...). A less formal way is to say *Questo è ...* (for a man) or *Questa è ...* (for a woman):

Questo è il mio amico Giorgio.
This is my friend George.
Questa è la mia amica Anna.
This is my friend Ann.

When introduced you always shake hands, and the standard remark is *Piacere* (Pleased to meet you).

Mi scusi, chi è lei?	Excuse me, who are you?
Di dov 'è lei?	Where are you from?
Sono … (give your name)	I am …
Sono di … (give name of your home town)	I am from …

Sono inglese	I am English
scozzese	Scottish
irlandese	Irish
gallese	Welsh
americano/a	American
australiano/a	Australian

Come si chiama?	What is your name?
Mi chiamo Jane.	My name is Jane.
Sono americana.	I am American.

Le piace = …You like	**Mi piace** = …I like
Le piace l'Italia?	Do you like Italy?
Sì. Mi piace molto.	Yes, I like it very much.
Le piace qui?	Do you like it here?
Sì. Mi piace l'albergo.	Yes. I like the hotel.
È molto comodo.	It's very comfortable.

In difficulty, you can say:

Che cosa? Come?	What? Pardon?
Non capisco.	I don't understand.
Non ricordo la parola.	I don't remember the word.
Non parlo italiano.	I don't speak Italian.
Parlo un po' di francese e tedesco.	I speak a bit of French and German.

For 'goodbye' use *buon giorno* or *buona sera* again, but late at night say *buona notte* (good night). *Arrivederci* (goodbye; literally 'see you again') is correct at any time. You may also hear the rather formal *arrivederla*.

*C*iao should be used only between friends and close acquaintances, or with children and young people. Note that it means both 'hello' and 'goodbye'.

A presto.	See you soon.
A domani.	See you tomorrow.
Grazie mille.	Thank you so much ('a thousand thanks').
È stata una bella giornata.	It was a lovely day.
Grazie della bellissima serata.	Thank you for the wonderful evening.

Numbers & Time

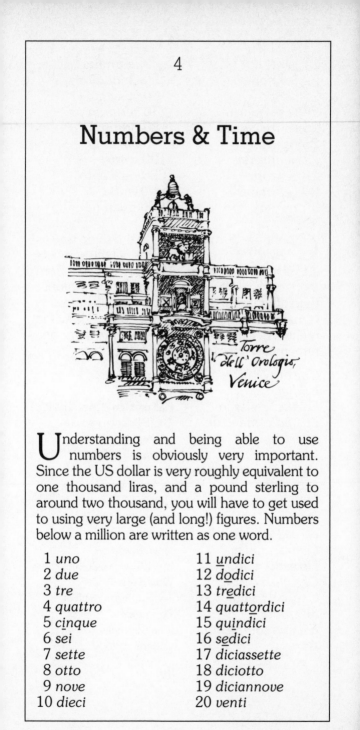

Torre dell' Orologio, Venice

Understanding and being able to use numbers is obviously very important. Since the US dollar is very roughly equivalent to one thousand liras, and a pound sterling to around two thousand, you will have to get used to using very large (and long!) figures. Numbers below a million are written as one word.

1 *uno*	11 *undici*
2 *due*	12 *dodici*
3 *tre*	13 *tredici*
4 *quattro*	14 *quattordici*
5 *cinque*	15 *quindici*
6 *sei*	16 *sedici*
7 *sette*	17 *diciassette*
8 *otto*	18 *diciotto*
9 *nove*	19 *diciannove*
10 *dieci*	20 *venti*

21 *ventuno*	40 *quaranta*
22 *ventidue*	50 *cinquanta*
23 *ventitré*	60 *sessanta*
24 *ventiquattro*	70 *settanta*
25 *venticinque*	80 *ottanta*
26 *ventisei*	90 *novanta*
27 *ventisette*	100 *cento*
28 *ventotto*	200 *duecento*
29 *ventinove*	1000 *mille*
30 *trenta*	2000 *duemila*

Count the 30s to the 90s in the same way as 20-29. To count the 100s put the numbers 2 to 9 in front of *cento*. 1000 is *mille*, but from then on is *mila*. One million is *un milione*, thereafter *milioni*. *Zero* is the same in Italian. ½ is *mezzo*, and ¼ is *quarto*. Once you know the numbers, telling the time is no problem; just remember to start with '*le —*' (see below).

Che ora è?	What time is it?
Le dieci.	Ten o'clock.
Le dieci e mezzo.	Half past ten ('ten and half').
Le undici meno un quarto.	10.45 ('eleven minus a quarter')
L'anno millenovecentonovantatré.	The year 1993.

Quanto costa?	How much does it cost?
Costa venticinquemila lire.	It costs 25,000 liras.
Quanti anni ha?	How old are you?
Ho ventisei anni.	I am 26 ('I have 26 years')
Che giorno è oggi?	What day is it today?
Oggi è il trenta dicembre.	Today is the thirtieth of December.
È il mio compleanno.	It's my birthday.
Auguri!	Congratulations!

The months of the year

genn<u>a</u>io	l<u>u</u>glio
febbr<u>a</u>io	agosto
marzo	settembre
aprile	ottobre
m<u>a</u>ggio	novembre
giugno	dicembre

F or the first of the month say *il primo*, otherwise use the numbers as given in the table.

Sono nato il trenta dicembre.	I was born on 30 December.
Anna è nata il primo aprile.	Anna was born on 1 April.

I giorni della settimana
(The days of the week)

luned<u>ì</u>	Monday
marted<u>ì</u>	Tuesday
mercoled<u>ì</u>	Wednesday
gioved<u>ì</u>	Thursday
venerd<u>ì</u>	Friday
s<u>a</u>bato	Saturday
dom<u>e</u>nica	Sunday

luned<u>ì</u> mattina	Monday morning
marted<u>ì</u> pomer<u>i</u>ggio	Tuesday afternoon
mercoled<u>ì</u> sera	Wednesday evening
gioved<u>ì</u> pr<u>o</u>ssimo	next Thursday
venerd<u>ì</u> scorso	last Friday
ogni s<u>a</u>bato	every Saturday
entro dom<u>e</u>nica notte	by Sunday night

Quando ci vediamo?	When shall we meet ('see each other')?
Ci vediamo domani sera verso le nove.	We'll meet tomorrow evening around nine.

Official national holidays in the Italian working calendar:

Capodanno:	(New Year's Day)
il primo gennaio.	
La Befana:	(Epiphany)
il 6 gennaio	
Lunedì dell' angelo	(Easter Monday)
('la pasquetta').	
L'anniversario della	(Liberation Day)
liberazione:	
il 25 aprile.	
La festa del lavoro:	(Labour Day)
il primo maggio.	
Ferragosto:	(August holiday, Feast of
il 15 agosto.	the Assumption)
Ognissanti:	(All Saints' Day)
il primo novembre.	
L'immacolata	(Immaculate Conception)
concezione:	
l'otto dicembre.	
Natale:	(Christmas Day)
il 25 dicembre.	
Santo Stefano:	(Boxing Day)
il 26 dicembre.	

In addition, every town celebrates its patron saint's day as a local holiday. For instance, no bank will be open in Milan on 7 December, for the feast of St Ambrose. For the first two to three weeks of August, when the whole of Italy is on holiday, almost everything except the tourist industry ceases to function normally. Government offices, businesses, factories, and even shops, bars and restaurants (except in holiday resorts) close for all or part of the period, despite efforts to make small businessmen stagger their holidays.

WEIGHTS AND MEASURES

1 kilo=approximately 2lbs
1 metre=approximately 1 yard

Mille grammi fanno un chilo.	A thousand grammes make one kilo.
Cento centimetri fanno un metro.	A hundred centimetres make a metre.
Vorrei ...	I'd like ...
Vorrei due chili e mezzo di ...	I'd like two and a half kilos of ...

IN EMERGENCY

The emergency telephone number is 113 for police, doctor and ambulance. Members of the European Community (in possession of Form E111) are entitled to free use of the Italian Health Service. However, since the public health service can leave a lot to be desired, particularly in Southern Italy, it is advisable to take out a full-cover insurance policy that will give you access to private treatment and clinics.

For minor ailments a visit to the nearest farmacia (chemist's) will be quite sufficient, since an Italian chemist is a highly-qualified professional.

Hopefully you will never have to say anything like:

Ho perduto il passaporto.	I have lost my passport.
Mi hanno rubato la borsa[1]/il portafogli[2]/ la macchina fotografica[3].	My handbag[1]/purse[2]/camera[3] has been stolen.

5

Booking a Room

Here you are, telephoning a hotel to book a room:

Pronto.	Hello (on telephone).
Chi parla?	Who's that (speaking)?
È l'Albergo Flavio?	Is that the Hotel Flavio?
Sì. Cosa desidera?	Yes. What can I do for you?
Vorrei una camera per quattro notti.	I would like a room for four nights.
Va bene. Per quando?	Alright. For when?
Dal ventotto al trentuno luglio.	From 28 to 31 July.
Una camera doppia o singola?	A double or single room?
Doppia. Con balcone possibilmente.	Double. With balcony if possible.
A due letti o matrimoniale?	With twin beds or double-bed?
Con bagno o doccia?	With bathroom or shower?
Matrimoniale, con bagno, per piacere.	Double-bed, with bathroom, please.

Benissimo. A che ora arriva?	Very well. What time will you be arriving?
Arriviamo la sera alle venti.	We'll be arriving at eight ('twenty') in the evening.

Note the use of the 24-hour clock. You could also say: *Arriviamo la sera alle otto.* Except for *all'una* (at one o'clock) *a mezzogiorno* (at midday) *a mezzanotte* (at midnight), 'at' expressing the time is always *alle …*

Quando parte il pullman per Napoli?	When does the coach for Naples leave?
*Parte **alle** sedici e trenta, e arriva **alle** diciotto e cinquanta.*	It leaves at 16.30, and arrives at 18.50.

Many guidebooks list recommended hotels. In Italy itself, tourist offices supply meticulous lists of accommodation, with up-to-date details of prices and facilities. Write to the *Ente Provinciale del Turismo* (provincial Tourist Office) in the main town nearest the locality of your choice, or in your own country contact the Italian State Tourist Office. Address a letter confirming a booking to *la direzione* (manager's office) of the hotel. In this kind of letter there is no section beginning 'Dear …'

Confermo la mia prenotazione di una camera doppia con bagno dal 27 al 31 luglio.	I confirm my booking of a double room with bath from 27 to 31 July.
Distinti saluti …	Yours faithfully …
un albergo di lusso	a luxury hotel
una pensione	a guesthouse
'camere libere'	'vacancies'
'completo'	'no vacancies'
il campeggio	campsite
la roulotte	caravan
la tenda	tent

Wherever you stay, on arrival you must register, a process known as *la certificazione*. Your particulars (*generalità*) will be transcribed from a personal document and notified to the local authorities.

cognome, nome	surname, name
nazionalità	nationality
luogo/data di nascita	place/date of birth
indirizzo	address

Useful vocabulary when staying in a hotel:

l'acqua calda/fredda	hot water/cold
il sapone	soap
l'asciugamano	towel
la carta igienica	toilet-paper
la chiave	the key
l'aria condizionata	air-conditioning
il riscaldamento	heating
la direzione, il bureau	hotel office
alta/bassa stagione	high/low season
il numero della camera	room number
il prezzo della camera	price of the room
Iva ed imposta soggiorno	VAT and tourist tax
inclusa	included

(By law hotel charges must be posted in each room)

6

Buon Appetito!

a more interesting experience

la colazione	breakfast
il pranzo	lunch
la cena	supper

Breakfast is invariably very light. For many Italians it is simply a quick cup of coffee. Breakfast is not included in the price of a room, unless you are paying *mezza pensione* (half board) or *pensione completa* (full board). In any case, it will only be a pot of coffee and some bread and jam, so you might have a more interesting experience (and probably better coffee) if you call at a nearby bar. Here you can get a fresh croissant (*un cornetto*) or a sweet pastry (*una pasta*), a roll (*un panino*), a toasted sandwich (*un tost*) or *una pizzetta*, pizza-bread filled with sliced mozzarella cheese and ham or salami (*salame* to Italians). There is no need to know all the words. Just point and say:

Prendo questo, e due di questi.
I'll take this, and two of these/those.

I taly has a great coffee culture, so you will have to specify:

un caff<u>è</u>	a small strong black 'espresso' coffee
un caff<u>è</u> lungo	a weak espresso (more water in it)
un caff<u>è</u> freddo	an iced coffee
un caff<u>è</u> macchiato	an espresso with a drop of milk
un cappuccino, un cappu<u>c</u>cio	an espresso with hot frothy milk
un caffellatte	a milk coffee, milkier than cappuccino

T he Italian preference is for an *espresso* or *caffellatte* in the morning, ordered in this way from the barman:

Mi fa (lit: make me) *due espressi e un caffellatte.*

I t is not felt impolite to omit 'please' (*per favore, per piacere, per cortesia*) when making predictable requests in normal circumstances. If you do not want the barman to sugar your drink, let him know before it is too late:

Senza zucchero.   Without sugar.

I t is nice to take your time and sit down at a table and watch the world go by, but if there is waiter service you should be warned that you will pay as much as two or three times the normal price. A price list (*il listino prezzi*) is prominently displayed, and should show prices *al banco* (at the counter) and *al tavolo* (at a table). The *al banco* routine is that you first pay at the till (*la cassa*) then take your receipt (*lo scontrino*) to the bar, handing it to the barman and telling him what you have paid for.

Un tè, tre cappuccini e quattro paste.
One tea, three cappuccinos, and four pastries.
Il tè al latte, non al limone, grazie.
Tea with milk, not with lemon, thanks.
Prego, signore.
Very good, sir.

The response to *grazie* is always *prego*: (You're welcome).

B ars are open from early morning until late at night. Most have an available toilet (*il gabinetto, la toilette*) and a public telephone (*il telefono*). Many also sell cigarettes and matches (*le sigarette, i fiammiferi*), postcards and stamps (*le cartoline, i francobolli*), as well as tickets for local transport services.

Prendiamo qualcosa (da bere)?	Shall we have something (to drink)?
Certo. Che cosa prende lei?	Sure. What will you have ('take')?
Prendo una birra, ma il bambino vuole un gelato.	I'll have a beer, but the little boy wants an ice cream.
Quanto fa?	How much does it come to?
Non importa, offro io.	It doesn't matter, I'm offering.
Salute! Cin cin!	Cheers!
Auguri!	All the best! Good luck!

Il pranzo (lunch) is the main meal of the day in Italy. Since shops and most businesses close for the early afternoon, and school is only in the morning, the whole family can be reunited round the lunch table, and there is even time to sleep it off after, with a short *siesta*. *Pranzo* is also the word for a formal dinner, and a full *pranzo* is a very substantial meal. *La cena* is lighter, for instance with soup or broth rather than *pastasciutta* (pasta with a sauce). No other Europeans dine out as frequently as the Italians.

Here are the main items in a typical *pranzo* menu:

Antipasto	starter, hors d'oeuvres
Primo piatto	'first course', pasta or soup (*la minestra*)
Secondo piatto	'second course', meat (*la carne*) or fish (*il pesce*)
Contorno	side-dish, vegetable or salad (*l'insalata*)
Dolce	sweet, dessert
Formaggio	cheese
Frutta	fruit
Caffè	coffee
Vino bianco o rosso	white or red wine

In a restaurant you pay VAT tax (*IVA*) on top of the cost of the food, and a quite substantial charge is also levied for *pane e coperto*, i.e. bread and cover charge. *Servizio*, the waiter's tip (5% is about right), is usually left up to the customer. Italians normally only order one side dish, sometimes following the *secondo*. Potatoes do not arrive as a matter of course, instead there is an abundance of bread (eaten without butter).

Names for meats: *manzo* (beef), *vitello* (veal), *maiale* (pork), *agnello* (lamb), *castrato* (mutton), *pollo* (chicken). Water, usually bottled mineral water, is considered a more essential accompaniment than wine. Ask for plain *acqua minerale naturale*, or *gasata* (fizzy). You should have a very satisfying meal if you ask for *i piatti del giorno* (chef's specialities of the day) and *il vino della casa* (the house wine).

Cameriere! Mi porti mezzo litro di bianco!
Waiter! Bring me a half-litre of white (wine)!

As for places to choose from, a *ristorante* is generally larger and more expensive than a *trattoria*, which is traditionally a family-run middle-priced restaurant. If you have to count your liras, first consult the menu if displayed outside, as there exist some very pricey fashionable *trattorie, osterie* and *taverne*.

A *pizzeria* should have a big wood-burning pizza oven, and usually has very reasonable prices. A *rosticceria* is a sort of high standard take-away, with spit-roasted meats and choice pre-cooked dishes. A *tavola calda* is a modest food bar. *Vino e cucina* is very basic, the wine more than the food being the interest.

Cucina casalinga is a sign to look for, promising good unfussy 'home-cooking'. A *menu turistico* or *prezzo fisso* (set price meal) is not to be recommended unless you cannot afford better.

The sandwich bar (*paninoteca*) and fast food shops like McDonald's are gaining enormous popularity. With the recent arrival of large numbers of non-European immigrants other types of cuisine, notably Chinese and Indian, are becoming quite widely available in the bigger cities.

Every second street in Italy seems to have an *alimentari* shop, a friendly, well-stocked grocery store that also sells fresh bread, wine and anything else you need for a simple picnic. At no extra charge they will cheerfully prepare sandwiches for you. To say what you want them 'with' use *al* for masculine and *alla* for feminine ingredients:

*Mi fa due panini; uno **al** form<u>a</u>ggio e uno **alla** mortadella.*

Make me two rolls; one with cheese and one with mortadella.

*Vorrei un gelato **al** limone e due **alla** fragola.*
I'd like a lemon icecream and two strawberry-flavoured.

C'è=there is   **Ci sono**=there are

C'è un tavolo libero?	Is there a table free?
C'è uno per quattro persone.	There's one for four people.
Ci sono piatti vegetariani?	Are there vegetarian dishes?
No, mi dispiace, non ci sono.	No, I'm sorry, there are not.
Andiamo dentro o fuori?	Shall we go inside or outside?
Preferisco mangiare fuori.	I prefer to eat outside.
È buona la bistecca?	Is the steak good?
Sì, è ottima.	Yes, it's excellent.
Vuole ancora un po' di vino?	Do you want a little more wine?
No, grazie, basta così.	No, thanks, that's enough.
Il conto, per piacere!	The bill/check, please!
Subito, signore!	Coming ('at once'), sir!
Ecco il resto.	Here's the change.
Tenga pure.	Please keep it. (Said when you tip)
Buon appetito!	Enjoy the meal!
Grazie, altrettanto.	Thank you, same to you.

7

Very Simple Guesswork: Words & Gestures

Italian is a development from Latin

So many words are guessable! Italian is a development from Latin, and many English words, especially the longer ones, also derive from Latin. Consequently both languages have a large stock of words of common origin. So if you are stuck for a word you can often make a well-informed guess at what it might be in Italian. With most such words only small adjustments are needed to make the change from one language to the other, most often in the way the word ends.

It should not be difficult for you to recognise the Italian equivalents, once your ear is accustomed to how the language is sounded. A few of these words are even identical. Spend a few minutes studying the following list and you will find that in almost no time at all you have acquired a potentially immense Italian vocabulary.Words are listed according to the way they end, with the Italian opposite the English.

ENGLISH	ITALIAN
-A idea, panorama	-A idea, panorama
-ABLE notable, favourable	-EVOLE, notevole, favorevole
-AL special, sandal	-ALE -ALO speciale, sandalo
-AM(MME) telegram, programme	–AMMA telegramma, programma
-ANCE fragrance, ambulance	–ANZA fragranza, ambulanza
-ANT elegant, deodorant	-ANTE elegante, deodorante
-ARY elementary, ordinary	-ARE -ARIO elementare, ordinario
-ATE fortunate, immediate	-ATO fortunato, immediato
-CAL typical, ecological	-CO tipico, ecologico
-ECT perfect, respect	-ETTO perfetto, rispetto
-ENCE -ENCY science, emergency	-ENZA scienza, emergenza
-IBLE terrible, possible	-IBILE terribile, possibile
-ID placid, invalid	-IDO placido, invalido
-ILE fertile, automobile	-ILE fertile, automobile
-ISM tourism, enthusiasm	-ISMO turismo, entusiasmo
-IST tourist, artist	-ISTA turista, artista†

-IVE active, initiative	-IVO -IVA attivo, iniziativa
-MENT moment, element	MENTO momento, elemento
-ONY matrimony, harmony	-ONIO -ONIA matrimonio, armonia
-O radio, stereo	-O radio, stereo
-OR -OUR superior, colour	-ORE superiore, colore
-ORY memory, history	-ORIA memoria, storia
-OUS curious, scandalous	-OSO curioso, scandaloso
-PHY geography, philosophy	-FIA geografia, filosofia
-SION version, decision	-SIONE versione, decisione
-SIS crisis, analysis	-ISI crisi, analisi
-TION emotion, station	-ZIONE emozione, stazione
-TY difficulty, quality	TÀ difficoltà, qualità
-URE future, temperature	-URO -URA futuro, temperatura

(† This type of word, although ending in -A, can also be masculine: *il dentista*, the dentist.)

Do not expect the above patterns to apply in every case. 'Sentiment' is *sentimento*, but 'contentment' is not 'contentimento' (it is *contentezza*). Also, when an Italian word sounds like it must have the identical meaning in English this is not necessarily so. *Pavimento* means floor, *morbido* means soft. Still, the table works in hundreds and hundreds of cases, so do not be discouraged.

Even if they do not fit into any of the above categories, you soon find that for various reasons a great many other Italian words easily stick in the memory, once you have met them. E.g. *lungo* (long), *difficile* (difficult), *numero* (number), *interesse* (interest), *strada* (street), *odore* (smell), *velocità* (speed).

A further help is the fact that many Italian **verbs** are more or less identical to the English. It is not too hard to guess what these mean: *abbandonare, adorare, celebrare, decidere, divorziare, finanziare, garantire, invitare, organizzare, preparare, visitare.*

The letters 'x' and 'y' in English are generally 's' and 'i' in Italian: *esperto, esistenza, stile, ritmo* (expert, existence, style, rhythm). The last example demonstrates that some English combinations of letters do not occur in Italian. For instance, there is no 'th' 'ph' 'pt' 'ct' 'bs'. Instead you find: *teatro* (theatre), *foto* (photo), *scultore* (sculptor), *fatto* (fact), *assurdo* (absurd).

GESTURES

Could you get by in Italy with no words at all? The hands, in fact the whole body, are an indispensable resource for many Italians, much as they were for Toscanini. So when you are lost for a word or expression there is no reason to be shy of resorting to a little graphic sign-language of your own. Some Italians hardly gesture at all, while others' hands are never still.

Observe people in conversation and you will soon notice that each has his or her own idiosyncratic way of 'conducting' a conversation. One while speaking will seem to be endlessly kneading dough, another winding wool, another forever rattling an imaginary pinball machine, another tightening a lid or wringing out a wet cloth, another trying to fit a key into a lock just in front of his nose …

Some gestures are specific to a certain region, such as the South Italian 'no' (a tut of the tongue, with head jerked *upwards*), others are common to the whole nation, so it is not advisable to copy them until you are sure what they are all about, or when it may be appropriate to use them. Here are a few widely used gestures to recognise. I offer only one 'translation', but this kind of body-talk is actually capable of many shades of meaning.

○ Dig a straight forefinger into your own cheek, then give it a half twist: **Fantastic!**
○ Waggle a raised forefinger from side to side, palm outwards: **No way!**
○ Lay both forefingers horizontally side by side, pointing the same way: **They're close friends.**

○ Point both forefingers straight at each other, then bump fingertips: **They're like cat and dog.**

○ Lock forefingers, and pull tight: **They're hand in glove.**

○ Clench the hand with thumb pressed against cheekbone, then draw down lower eyelid: **Smart guy!**

○ Same gesture, but using forefinger: **Watch out!**

○ Raise hands slackly in 'I surrender' pose, level with ears: **Search me!**

○ Shake hand (even both hands) with the fingertips bunched against the thumbpad, palm up: **What's the matter?**

○ Hands lowered with fingertips interlaced, moved up and down: **Who are you kidding?**

○ Loosely shape forefinger and thumb like a revolver, and oscillate from wrist: **No such luck!**

○ Draw a horizontal line before your chest, with palm inward and forefinger and thumb pinched together: **Perfect!**

○ Cock both thumbs and shake your hands (turned inwards) vigorously from the wrist: **I can't take any more!**

○ With all fingers parallel drive your right hand hard between left thumb and forefinger a couple of times: **Beat it!**

○ For catching a waiter's attention you raise your hand with the thumb and next two fingers spread and then 'tremble' the hand from side to side. The word to call out is '*Senta!*'

A ll gestures of course to be accompanied by an appropriate facial expression!

8

Sightseeing, Shopping, Entertainment

Scooting at Stra

Any sightseeing which is to include museums, galleries etc. should be planned for the morning, as they will almost certainly be closed for the rest of the day. Very few will be open at all on a Monday. Churches reopen their doors towards evening. Notable exceptions, in the summer months, are the Vatican Museums and the Uffizi Gallery in Florence, which keep later hours. Archaeological sites stay open until around sundown, but they too remain shut all day Monday. Various reductions operate in most of these places.

chiuso/aperto	closed/open
giorni feriali	weekdays
orario festivo	timetable for Sundays and holidays
gli scavi	excavations
il museo	museum

la galleria	gallery
la pinacoteca	picture gallery
l'ingresso/l'uscita	entrance/exit
il biglietto d'ingresso	entrance ticket
Quando apre/chiude?	When does it open/close?

SHOPPING

Shops operate an eight-hour day, but with a long break in the middle. Open hours are generally 9 a.m.-1 p.m., then 3.30-7.30 p.m. Sales are announced by notices such as *Saldi, Svendita, Sconto 50%* (50% off everything). At markets, which can start as early as 8 a.m., bartering is the norm.

Solo cinquemila, signora!	Only 5,000, madam!
Scherza?	Are you joking?
È troppo.	It's too much.
Non mi fa uno sconto?	Won't you take something off?
Beh, facciamo quattromila.	Well, let's make it 4,000.
Eh no, tremilacinque e basta!	Oh no, 3,500, and that's it!

(*Cento* is very often left out when talking of prices.)

Dove=where   **Dov'è ...?**=where is? ...

Dove posso comprare un/una ...?	Where can I buy a ...?
Dov'è il supermercato?	Where is the supermarket?
Sa dov'è una lavanderia?	Do you know where there's a laundry?
Sì, lei deve andare sempre diritto, e poi girare a destra/ sinistra quando arriva alla seconda traversa.	Yes, you have to go straight on, and then turn right/ left when you come to the second crossing.

*Scusi, cerco
una farmacia e un
negozio di giocattoli.*

Excuse me, I'm looking for
a chemist's and a
toyshop.

Here are words you will see on shopfronts, or places you might want to ask for. (When asking, you will need to put '*un negozio di ...*' in front of the words asterisked.)

*Abbigliamento	clothing
Barbiere	barber's
Calzoleria	shoe shop
Cartoleria	stationer's
Coiffeur	ladies' hairdresser
*Confezione	clothing store
Erboristeria	herbalist's
Farmacia	chemist's
*Ferramenta	hardware
Fioraio	florist
Fotografo	photographer's
*Giocattoli	toyshop
Gioielleria	jeweller's
Lavanderia	laundry
Libreria	bookshop
*Moda	fashion shop, boutique
Oreficeria	goldsmith's
*Ottica	optician
Parrucchiere	hairdresser
Tabaccheria	tobacconist
Tintoria	cleaner's
Ufficio postale	post office
*Alimentari	food store
Bottiglieria	wine-shop
Drogheria	grocery
Enoteca	wine merchant
Fruttivendolo	greengrocer
Gelateria	ice cream parlour
Latteria	dairy
Macelleria	butcher
Panetteria	baker's

Panificio	baker's
Pasticceria	confectioner's
Pastificio	pasta maker's
Pescheria	fishmonger
Pizziccheria	delicatessen
Polleria	poultry shop
Salumeria	pork butcher
Salsamenteria	delicatessen
Vinaio	wine-shop

Desidera? Dica?	Can I help you?

Ha un pacchetto/una scatola/una bottiglia/un paio di ...?
Do you have a packet/tin, or box/bottle/pair of ...?
No, ma abbiamo questo, o vuole questo qui?
No, but we have this, or do you want this one here?
È brutto, e anche troppo caro. Voglio questo.
It's ugly, and also too dear. I want this one.

Più grande,	Larger,
meno grande?	or less large?
Più piccolo, o così?	Smaller, or like this?
Di che colore?	What colour?
Bianco, nero, rosso,	White, black, red,
verde, marrone	green, brown
giallo, azzurro, rosa	yellow, blue, pink
grigio, arancione	grey, orange
di lana, seta, cotone	in wool, silk, cotton
E poi? Altro?	And next? Anything else?
Sì, un sacchetto.	Yes, a carrier bag.
Quanto fa in tutto?	How much is it altogether?
Fa diecimila-cinquecento.	That is L.10,500.

M any food items, even bread or a slice of pizza, will be weighed in front of you. Note that *un etto* means 100 grams.

Basta così, signora? O facciamo due etti?
Is that enough, madam? Or shall we make it 200 grams?

to make
Fare: *io* FACCIO *noi* FACCIAMO *lui, lei* FA
to go
Andare: VADO *noi* ANDIAMO *lui, lei* VA

Che cosa fa questa sera?	What are you doing this evening?
Più tardi vado in discoteca.	Later I'm going to a discotheque.
Facciamo una passeggiata ora?	Shall we take a walk now?
Sì, e poi andiamo a mangiare.	Yes, and then let's go to eat.
Facciamo così?	Shall we do that?
D'accordo.	Okay ('agreed').

Before the evening meal most of the town parades up and down the main street for the evening stroll, *la passeggiata* or *lo struscio* (the shuffle!). Pavement cafés are packed in the warmer months. Red watermelons (*cocomeri*) are on sale everywhere. Dance bands play outside, there are open-air cinemas, concerts, plays and street *feste*. (*Festa* is also the word for a party.) Entertainments, exhibitions, sporting events are prominently advertised on walls all over town. But note that all foreign films are dubbed into Italian. Opera houses are not open in summer, but there are many music festivals, and of course the great open-air opera spectacles at the Arena in Verona and the Baths of Caracalla in Rome.

Quando comincia lo spettacolo?
When does the show begin?

9

Getting Around

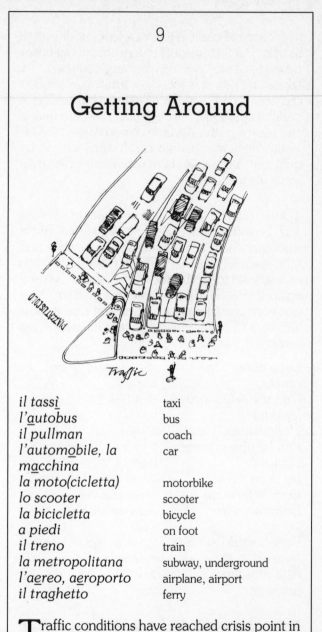

Traffic

il tass<u>ì</u>	taxi
l'<u>a</u>utobus	bus
il pullman	coach
l'autom<u>o</u>bile, la	car
m<u>a</u>cchina	
la moto(cicletta)	motorbike
lo scooter	scooter
la bicicletta	bicycle
a piedi	on foot
il treno	train
la metropolitana	subway, underground
l'a<u>e</u>reo, a<u>e</u>roporto	airplane, airport
il traghetto	ferry

Traffic conditions have reached crisis point in all of Italy's bigger cities, so consider taking the *metropolitana* (also known, as *il metrò*) if stations are conveniently situated. A good way to get around easily is to hire a scooter, or even a bicycle. Public transport is very cheap, but buses have few seats and can be very crowded. To take a taxi-ride in Naples is as thrilling as a roller-coaster. It can be a nightmare trying to find a parking space (*un parcheggio*) anywhere near a city centre in the daytime. Never leave possessions visible in a parked car. Italians who value their car radios take them with them when they leave the vehicle.

Bus tickets have to be bought before boarding, then on the bus inserted into a machine which stamps them with the date and time to cancel them (*l'obliterazione*). They are usually valid for an hour or more, so can be used again if you have to change bus or tram. You can purchase them at a tobacconist's or at most bars or a newspaper kiosk (*l'edicola*) beside the route.

Devo andare in centro.	I have to go to the city centre.
Quant'è (=Quanto+è) lontano?	How far is it?
È abbastanza vicino.	It's fairly near.
Perché non prende l'autobus?	Why don't you take the bus?
Da dove parte?	Where does it leave from?
Ecco la fermata.	There's the stop.
Entrata/uscita	entrance/exit (on bus or train)
Dove scendo per San Pietro?	Where do I get off for St Peter's?
Alla prossima fermata.	At the next stop.

In a crush, watch out for pickpockets, and like your fellow-passengers be prepared to call out *Permesso!* (Excuse me) or *Scendo!* (I'm getting off here) to clear a path to the exit.

If travelling a long distance by train buy food beforehand, as restaurant and buffet cars are rare and the corridor trolleys are very expensive. It is well worth paying the extra *supplemento* for a *super-rapido* or *rapido* (express train), or book ahead on the fast and efficient Inter-City trains. In this case there is no extra charge for a seat reservation. Other trains tend to dawdle, but they are more punctual than is popularly supposed.

Un biglietto di prima/seconda classe.
First/second-class ticket.

Semplice/andata e ritorno.
Single/return (ticket).

Due, Roma, solo andata.
Two tickets for Rome, one way only.

Quando parte il prossimo treno per …?
When does the next train leave for …?

È in orario, è in ritardo?
Is it on time, is it late?

È necessario prenotare?
Is it necessary to book?

Vorrei prenotare un posto a sedere/una cuccetta.
I'd like to book a seat/a couchette.

A che ora è la coincidenza per …?
At what time is the connection for …?

Devo cambiare a Bologna?
Do I have to change in Bologna?

Da che binario parte?
Which platform does it go from?

La biglietteria	ticket office
arrivi/partenze	arrivals/departures
la carrozza ristorante	restaurant-car
vicino al finestrino	next to the window
il vagone letto	wagon-lits
il deposito bagagli	left-luggage office
la sala d'attesa	waiting-room
sottopassaggio	underpass

B esides Sardinia and Sicily, there are scores of islands around Italy's long coastline which are served by ferryboat and hydrofoil (*aliscafo*). If travelling by car, be warned that in the high season there can be long queues, especially from mainland ports to Sardinia, so it is advisable to book well in advance. Particularly convenient, if you want to cut out a long train or car journey, is the Naples-Sicily ferry service. There are good internal flights which are heavily used for the otherwise lengthy journeys between the north and south of Italy.

T his is the sign for a tourist information office (*ufficio informazioni*) at airports, major stations and in town centres. Apart from time-table information, it will probably have a useful town plan to give you (*una piantina della città*), and also advice on accommodation.

DRIVING

C ar hire (*autonoleggio*) is very costly but necessary if you like the independence and hope to explore off the beaten track. By law you must carry a warning triangle in the car, in case of breakdown. In trouble, the first words you need are *autosoccorso* (breakdown service) and *autoservizio*, a garage that can cope with anything from a flat tyre (*una gomma a terra*) to engine repairs (*riparazioni al motore*). An *autofficina* is similar but smaller, while an *elet-*

tr<u>au</u>to will see to electrical faults. When filling up, the choice is between high or low octane *benzina* (petrol, gas): *super* or *normale*. Not many filling stations are automated.

Sa dov'è il pr<u>o</u>ssimo distributore?
Do you know where the nearest filling-station is?
È a tre chil<u>o</u>metri da qui.
It's three kilometres from here.
Mi fa il pieno di super, per favore.
Fill up with 'super', please.
Devo controllare l'<u>o</u>lio.
I need to check the oil.
Acqua, gomme a posto?
Water, tyres okay?
Tutto a posto, gr<u>a</u>zie.
Everything okay, thanks.

D rivers must carry all vehicle documents with them. Speed limits are 50km in built-up areas, 90km on the open road, and 130km on the *autostrada* (motorway). Front-seat passengers must wear seat-belts. Latest figures on how many were wearing seat-belts when involved in accidents are very revealing about regional attitudes to rules and regulations: 61% in the North, 38% in the Centre, 12% in the South.

A fine (*una multa*) will be very high, but cheaper if paid on the spot. If stopped by the *carabinieri* or *polizia stradale* (traffic police) you may be asked to produce:
la patente, il libretto, l'assicurazione, la carta verde
driving licence, logbook, insurance, green card.

R oad signs to note in particular:

senso <u>u</u>nico   one way street
rallentare   slow down
alt/avanti   stop/go

entrata/uscita	entrance/exit
deviazione	diversion
limite di velocità	speed limit
parcheggio	parking
divieto di sosta	no parking
zona rimozione	car parked here will be
(or *rimozione forzata*)	towed away (to be re-claimed at considerable cost).

The *autostrada* network is excellent and well-maintained, and now extends over the whole peninsula and Sicily. But you have to pay a toll (*pedaggio*). At the control point press the red button for your ticket (*scontrino*), to be handed in at the exit point where an electronic screen shows the charge and any change (*saldo*) due. Hitch-hiking is forbidden on an *auto-strada*. Finally, do not forget that in Italy:

Deve guidare a destra.	You must drive on the right.
Buon viaggio!	Safe journey!

TELEPHONING

Public telephones take coins or special metal tokens (*i gettoni*), which you can buy at the *cassa* in a bar, or from a newsagents. Put them in before lifting the receiver. For a long-distance call you will need to feed in a lot of coins, your change being returned when you hang up. A *gettone* is worth L200 and is often given as change in place of the equivalent coin.

Fortunately, the phonecard system is now being widely introduced and it is obviously much more convenient for a long-distance call (*una telefonata interurbana*) or an interna-tional call (*una telefonata internazionale*). A phonecard (*una carta telefonica*) is bought from a tobacconist's. Note that the phonecard will not work unless you first tear off (*strappare*) the top right-hand corner. Every town has its *ufficio della SIP* (pronounced 'seep'), the State Telephone Office, where they can put through calls for you.

Posso telefonare?	Can I use the telephone?
Devo telefonare in Inghilterra.	I have to telephone England.
Voglio telefonare per un tassì.	I want to 'phone for a taxi.

to be able, 'can'
Potere: *io* POSSO *noi* POSSIAMO *lui, lei* PUÒ
to have to, 'must'
Dovere: DEVO DOBBIAMO DEVE
to want
Volere: VOGLIO VOGLIAMO VUOLE

These three indispensable verbs are 'irregular', that is even the first sound of the verb changes. But the endings (except for *può*) follow the normal pattern. They are important to learn because you can devise so many useful phrases with them. They are very easy to use, because they are always followed by a verb in its simple infinitive form:

Devo pagare.	I must pay.
Dobbiamo andare.	We must go.
Non vuole partire.	He doesn't want to leave.
Vogliamo vedere il Colosseo.	We want to see the Coliseum.
Voglio mangiare un bel piatto di pasta.	I want to eat a nice (big) plate of pasta.
Non posso aspettare.	I can't wait.

10

Banks and Business

The Pirelli tower, Milan

Precise opening hours for banks vary widely, but certainly all are open mornings Monday to Friday between 9 a.m. and 1 p.m. Later in the afternoon they will reopen for one hour, usually 2.30-3.30 p.m., sometimes 3-4 p.m. For any transaction remember to bring your passport or another identity document.

If you need cash out of banking hours, an exchange bureau (*cambio*) operates the same opening hours as the local shops. Entering a bank (and also consulates and embassies) can be like entering some mini-Fort Knox, with a gun-toting guard outside and a sealed security chamber to pass through. But this is routine and everyone is very relaxed inside. Make for the foreign desk (*cambio* again), where very likely no one's English will be much better than your Italian.

Devo incassare	I have to cash
questo assegno.	this cheque.
Vorrei cambiare	I'd like to change
questi soldi in	this money into
lire italiane.	Italian liras.
L'indirizzo, il numero	Your address, your passport
del passaporto e	number and
la firma, per piacere.	signature, please.
il dollaro, la sterlina.	US dollar, British pound.
il cambio del giorno.	Today's exchange rate.

The clerk who deals with your cheque or card is not the same one who issues cash. He will hand you a copy of the transaction which you then have to take to the *cassa* (cashier's counter) where you will get your *documento* back and receive your cash. Some large central banks now have cash-points available to VISA card-holders.

A business trip to Italy will obviously be carefully prepared, with itinaries worked out and meetings set up in advance. Nevertheless, most executives, unlike some state-sector officials whom you may have to deal with, will prove very flexible, and impromptu arrangements in both parties' interest are easily accommodated.

At the meeting (*la riunione* or *il meeting*) your opposite number will almost certainly be as uneasy as yourself about doing business in another language. Even if his or her English is quite good, the preference will be to use an interpreter when round the negotiating table, or to bring in an English-speaking colleague.

As well as an air of professional expertise, the ability to appear relaxed and friendly will aid the reception of your point of view. Be open to exchanges on non-business matters, as Italians like to know you are a person too! Large companies have their own bars on the premises, and a coffee or a shared bottle of beer will be part of the warm-up process. Any effort at small-talk in Italian should be well-received, and in any case Italians in the same field of operations as yourself will be pretty familiar with a lot of the relevant English technical jargon.

On a more general level, you will find that a great many English terms especially to do with technology, commerce, sport and the media, are widely used in Italy today: *il computer, il marketing, gli hooligans, etc.*

Sono qui in vacanza/ per affari	I'm here on holiday/ on business
la società, la filiale	company, branch
l'agenzia	agency
l'azienda, la ditta	firm
l'orario d'ufficio	office hours
il proprietario, il padrone	the owner
l'amministratore delegato	managing director
il capoufficio	office manager
'il capo'	'boss'
il personale, il/la dipendente	staff, employee
il/la rappresentante	representative
la segretaria	secretary
il/la cliente	client, customer
il mio/la mia collega	my colleague
il suo/la sua collega	his/her/your colleague
Ecco il mio biglietto da visita	Here is my card
Sono qui a nome di …	I am here on behalf of …
Ho un appuntamento con … per le dieci.	I have an appointment with … for ten o'clock.
C'è il Dottor Bruni?	Is Dr Bruni in?
Mi dispiace, non c'è ma torna presto.	I'm sorry, he's not in but he'll be back soon.
Può aspettare?	Can you wait?
S'accomodi.	Take a seat.

11

Making Conversation

gondoliers waiting and chatting

to come
Venire: *io* VENGO *noi* VENIAMO *lui, lei* VIENE

Da dove viene?	Where do you come from?
Vengo da New York.	I come from New York.
Ma sono nato/a …	But I was born in …
Ho lavorato un anno	I worked a year
a Londra.	in London.
Dove lavora ora?	Where do you work now?
Che lavoro fa?	What's your job?
Faccio l'impiegato/a.	I'm an office-worker.
Sono un pensionato.	I'm retired.
<u>*Abita in città?*</u>	Do you live in town?
Abbiamo una casa in	We have a house in the
campagna e una villa	country and a villa
al mare.	by the sea.

Beato/a lei!	Aren't you lucky!	
Noi abbiamo solo un apartamento di quattro camere.	We only have a four-room flat.	
È sposato/a?	Are you married?	
Sono sposato/a da venti anni.	I have been married twenty years.	
Ha famiglia?	Do you have a family?	
Abbiamo tre bambini.	We have three children.	
Il più grande ha sedici anni.	The oldest (boy) is sixteen.	
La più piccola ha nove anni.	The youngest (girl) is nine.	
Le piace nuotare.	She likes swimming.	
Ecco una fotografia di ...	Here's a photo of ...	

mio	*marito*	husband
suo	*padre*	father
nostro	*figlio*	son
	fratello	brother
	cugino	cousin
	nonno	grandfather
	zio	uncle
mia	*moglie*	wife
sua	*madre*	mother
nostra	*figlia*	daughter
	sorella	sister
	cugina	cousin
	nonna	grandmother
	zia	aunt

mio/mia=my
suo/sua=his, her, your
nostro/nostra=our

By now you may be thinking that VERY SIMPLE ITALIAN is not really so simple … So here are a few things in conclusion which hopefully will give you more confidence in making conversation.

QUESTION WORDS

Che? Che cosa? Cosa?	What?
Chi?	Who?
Come?	How?
Dove?	Where?
Perché?	Why? (also 'because')
Quando?	When?
Quanto/a?	How much? How long?
Quanti/e?	How many?

When there is no question word, the speaker's intonation will indicate that a phrase is a question, usually by rising at the end.

A common way of turning a sentence into a question is to add: …, *VERO?* (true? right?):

L'italiano non è molto semplice, **vero**?
Italian isn't very simple, is it?

EXCLAMATIONS

Accidenti!	Damn!
Aiuto!	Help!
Appunto.	Exactly.
Auguri!	Good luck!
Basta!	That's enough!
Beh …	Well …
Boh!	I haven't a clue!
Complimenti!	Congratulations!
Dai!	Come on!

Dipende.	It depends.
Finalmente!	At last!
Forse.	Perhaps.
Forza!	Get on with it!
Macché!	No way!
Magari.	Perhaps. If only …
Mamma mia!	Good heavens!
Naturalmente.	Of course.
Pazienza!	Never mind!
Pazzesco!	Incredible!
Peccato!	What a pity!
Per carità!	God forbid!
Purtroppo.	Unfortunately.
Stupendo!	Wonderful!
Su!	Hurry up!

PAIRS/OPPOSITES

One way to make vital words stick in your memory is to learn to get to know them with their opposites:

allora/ora	then/now
con/senza	with/without
dentro/fuori	inside/outside
meglio/peggio	better/worse
più/meno	more/less
poco/molto	a little/a lot
poco/troppo	a little/too much
presto/tardi	early/late
prima/dopo	before/after
sempre/mai	always/never
solo/insieme	alone/together
sopra/sotto	above/below
tutti/nessuno	everyone/no one
tutto/niente	everything/nothing
vicino/lontano	near/far

COLOUR YOUR SPEECH: PAIRED ADJECTIVES

affascinante/noioso	fascinating/boring
allegro/malinconico	cheerful/melancholy
alto/basso	high/low
antico/moderno	ancient/modern
bello/brutto	beautiful/ugly
bravo/sciocco	clever/silly
buffo/serio	funny/serious
buono/cattivo	good/bad
caldo/freddo	hot/cold
caro/economico	dear/cheap
corto/lungo	short/long
dolce/amaro	sweet/bitter
facile/difficile	easy/difficult
felice/triste	happy/sad
forte/debole	strong/weak
furbo/fesso	sly/simple
gentile/scortese	kind/rude
giovane/vecchio	young/old
grande/piccolo	big/small
largo/lungo	wide/long
libero/occupato	free/engaged
pieno/vuoto	full/empty
primo/ultimo	first/last
pulito/sporco	clean/dirty
ricco/povero	rich/poor
simpatico/antipatico	nice/nasty
sveglio/stanco	alert/tired
utile/inutile	useful/useless
veloce/lento (piano)	fast/slow
vero/falso	true/false
vivace/pigro	lively/lazy

Che bello!	How lovely!
Che gentile!	How kind!
Che buffo!	How funny! etc.

An adjective is easily changed to an adverb (ends in -LY in English) by adding -*MENTE*:

veloce — *veloce**mente**:*
quick — quickly
But
a) If the adjective ends in -O, change to -A
b) If the adjective ends in -E, drop the -E
e.g. *ver**o*** — *ver**amente***
true — truly
*gentil**e*** — *gentil**mente***
kind — kindly
*regolar**e*** — *regolar**mente***
regular — regularly

… *Buon divertimento, specialmente in Italia!*
Have a good time, especially in Italy!